THE POWER OF OUR WORDS:

A Journey into the Power of Words
and the Impact They Have on All Life

LIZ MCGRATH

iUniverse, Inc.
New York   Bloomington

The Power of Our Words
A Journey into the Power of Words and
the Impact They Have on All Life

iUniverse books may be ordered through booksellers or by contacting:

iUniverse
1663 Liberty Drive
Bloomington, IN 47403
www.iuniverse.com
1-800-Authors (1-800-288-4677)

*Because of the dynamic nature of the Internet, any Web addresses or links
contained in this book may have changed since publication and may no longer be
valid. The views expressed in this work are solely those of the author and do not
necessarily reflect the views of the publisher, and the publisher hereby disclaims
any responsibility for them.*

ISBN: 978-1-4401-2299-6 (pbk)
ISBN: 978-1-4401-2300-9 (ebk)

Printed in the United States of America

iUniverse rev. date: 2/27/2009

This book is dedicated to everyone.

ACKNOWLEDGMENTS

I would like to extend my sincere appreciation and gratitude to my family, Samia, Michele Capra, Helen Miller, Lester Hedgecock, Don Bradley, and Stephen Steiner for their input, insights, encouragement, and support in assisting me in the birthing of this book: *The Power of Our Words.*

CONTENTS

INTRODUCTION

My quest for knowledge started at the age of fifteen when I made this statement to myself on the way to work one morning: *There must be more to life than what I am living.* I had a challenge thinking that my whole life would be the same, day in and day out.

At nineteen I enrolled in a yoga class and discovered viewpoints that definitely challenged mine. So before I took these on, I decided to investigate. This quest put me on a path of self-discovery.

From yoga I moved into the study of Chinese medicine—their philosophy and body movement such as tai chi and qigong. After a number of years studying the theory of Chinese medicine, I found that they devoted only one quarter of a page to emotions. I was quite confounded by this, as I felt that our emotions can trigger all sorts of things within us. I felt very strongly that emotions were the underlying cause for many things in our lives. I realized that I had learned everything I needed from these systems.

I was introduced to a chiropractor who specialized in the Mitzvah Technique. Through this practice, I started to awaken to the idea that I was totally in charge of my body and what happened to it. I was introduced to the wave motion in the spine. When initiated properly, the wave motion set about certain body dynamics in which I felt that I was being walked. It's quite a unique sensation.

At the same time that I was learning this method, I was asked by a friend to check out a belly dance class with her. I discovered that this activity was a continuation of my journey of self-discovery. The dancers were doing an undulating movement, which creates a wave motion in the spine. I was delighted. This pursuit led me into the Western philosophers and the ancient mysteries of Egypt.

During my sixteen years as a student and teacher of this amazing art form, I found the secret to the power of the belly dance, which provided a great bodywork to process my changes because it is geometrically based. This fell in line with my other studies in the ancient mysteries and sciences, which led me into various arenas and mystery schools such as The Rosicrucian Order AMORC, The Traditional Martinist Order, and The Builders of the Adytum (BOTA), taking me into deeper studies, which is still ongoing.

During my time learning about the Middle Eastern Oriental Dance, I met Stephen Steiner—a hypnotherapist and an eloquent communicator. One of his specialties is the field of cognitive restructuring. I loved listening to him and wanted very much to be able to express myself in like manner. This is where I truly learned the power of our words and the effect they had on each of us.

In the time I spent with him, I learned to articulate my thoughts and ideas through the proper use of words to make myself understood. Hence, I became more confident in my ability to communicate effectively.

It became apparent after each session what needed work. I was using negative words to describe positive things as well as describing what something was by what it wasn't. The task then, for me, was to learn how to say what something *is* in positive words. I had to rethink everything I was going to say and basically had to learn to speak all over again.

In this process, I found that I had to speak a lot less to give myself a chance to reorganize my thoughts to express them positively and clearly. Learning to say what *is* by using empowering words that convey the intended meaning was a challenging task to say the least.

I recognized that, in using cognitive restructuring, Stephen Steiner would resort to the use of repetitive phrases to help me get my mind on track. Sometimes he would ask me this question: If you are traveling between point A and point B, at what point can you take your eyes off the road or your hands off the wheel? The answer: With respect to taking your eyes off the road, hardly ever. Glancing in the rearview mirror to make a lane change or to pass someone was okay; however, we must always keep our eyes on the road ahead.

Here's another way of explaining this: It's all right to glance at the past; however, we need to be focused on the present in order to make the changes necessary to enhance our lives. The second part of the answer, referring to the point at which you take your hands off the wheel, is this: You take your hands off the wheel when you have parked the car and switched off the ignition.

After one of my sessions, I got the idea to make up a set of cards with the sayings and phrases Steiner used frequently, so that I would remember them. (I will share some of them with you further on in the book.) I then reinforced these phrases by daily repetition along with the practice of a mirror focus exercise he gave me to strengthen my mind. (This exercise will also be given to you later in this book.) This technique was most effective and beneficial. I highly recommend it.

One day the focus exercise became particularly challenging. My mind was incessantly bombarded with thoughts. The more I tried to focus my mind, the stronger and faster the thoughts came. I decided at that point to stop and examine my thoughts. I discovered that most of them were related to the past and the future.

The alarming fact was that I observed only two thoughts that concerned the present. With this realization, I concluded that I am very seldom in the here and now. It was apparent that the significance of this focus exercise along with the repetition of these phrases assisted me greatly to live more and more in the present moment. This was vital to the quality of my existence.

In just a short time, my life started to change. I felt as if I were coming out of a fog and into a new reality. I was more attuned to the here and now, simply observing what *is*. It became easier to speak about what *is*, because it was fact in evidence. This, in itself, was quite an awakening.

As my reasoning abilities were improving, I found myself questioning everything. This started an inner house cleaning and clearing. I questioned all of my thought patterns, belief systems, rules, clichés, and slogans in order to separate the wheat from the chaff and therefore to arrive at their intrinsic value. I asked myself if, in fact, they worked at all for me and, for that matter, for the people I adopted them from. As soon as I put my thoughts to the light of reasoning and intuition, I soon realized what had to go. The letting-go process became easier and made room for me to upgrade my operating system, so to speak.

Thus began the true journey of re-creating myself as the self I truly wanted to be and living the life I truly came here to live. Perhaps the re-creation or reconditioning process was simply remembering how to manifest my Divine Self.

I realized that the power behind this process began with the desire to understand and know my self. Using word cards as an oracle and carefully worded phrases, I continually cultivated, developed, and strengthened my goals and aspirations when doing the mirror focus exercise. Truly, I believed I had found a formula for life-altering change.

I started looking at life a whole lot differently. I realized that my life was in my own hands and that, with the proper inner direction, it could be what it was truly designed to be.

When I came across anything that expressed a great deal of wisdom, I formulated that wisdom as new goals, using carefully worded statements. My truest desire was to manifest as a spiritualized human being. To achieve this, I first had to learn what it meant to be human and learn to be the best I could be as a responsible citizen of the universe.

This particular goal is forever ongoing as I am always more than I was a moment ago. I am a being with a capacity to maximize an infinite potential, which is representative of the Divine Presence within.

When faced with a specific situation that placed me at a crossroads, I asked myself: *What would the Divine Presence, or God, think, say, and do in this situation?* As I thought about that, I then asked myself how I could begin to emulate the attributes of the Divine naturally? The answer came in the form of an intention that best fit my truest desire. It became the foundation and force behind the manifestation of everything in my life. It would govern all of my thoughts, words, actions, and deeds. This intention transformed my life and challenged my integrity, ethics, and motivations—in short, everything. It was a major uprooting.

The intention pointed to a desire to be in harmony with my true spiritual nature, to live in accordance with the cosmic intelligence and its laws for the highest good of all. This set the stage for learning to become a fully realized and spiritualized human being, becoming one with the All and being fully conscious of the process. A tall order I know, however, we all have the realm of infinity to achieve this aim.

Such a desire set forces into play that began a quickening process. I was grateful to have found a most profound power for change. I realized that what I knew was minuscule and that there was much more to learn. My world became all encompassing. I saw that my inner and outer worlds were fully connected. I began to understand that this intelligence is constantly communicating with us. Therefore, to be receptive to the message, we must be in the here and now. This realization had a huge impact on my life and, in a sense, made it easier and comforting to know I was in good company.

All this came about simply by implementing a few phrases made up of empowering words.

In this book, I present a chronology of the words used to effect change. The chronology deals with the definition of the words and how an investigation into their meaning can contribute to a powerful and worthy intention. I look at the power of suggestion at every level of communication and explain how all the points presented so far impact our mind and therefore our lives.

Through a brief investigation of the mind and its components, I offer you a way to strengthen your mind, enhance your level of concentration, gain new insights, and reinforce your goals through visualization. This practice can guide you to live a more fulfilling life.

The purpose of this book is to share what I have come to understand about the power of our words. This has been put to a rigorous testing in my own life as our family faced what seemed at times to be insurmountable situations. This process taught me to trust the greater power within. Because of this, my life and the lives of my family members were transformed and continue to be transformed to this day.

Using everyday words as a way of reconditioning works. I sincerely hope this practice is as helpful for you as it is for me and many others. I strongly feel that this new awareness can promote and contribute to various ways that will serve the highest good of all.

WORDS

In the Gospel according to St. John, chapter 1, the first line begins with "In the beginning was the word."

Words are made up of letters from an alphabet that constitutes the building blocks for our words. Words are part of a universal language; therefore, they carry an energy vibration.

Words, along with the images they create, are a direct line of communication with the subconscious mind. They are the template and prescription for the process of manifestation. Herein, as I understand it, is the true and full power of our words. This will be discussed further on.

Words can determine our feelings, our outlook on life, our perception of reality, and our thinking on a level of communication that propels us into action.

Words can completely uplift, delight, and catapult us into a desirable mental state that keeps us in the present moment, fully in charge and ready to act at a moment's notice.

Words are proactive in nature and can offer solutions. When the words we use are empowering, we and others also feel empowered.

Here are just a few ways we use words:

- ☐ To describe our thoughts, images, and feelings
- ☐ To communicate a message.
- ☐ To express ourselves
- ☐ To communicate and interact with others
- ☐ To associate certain events in our lives
- ☐ To associate meaning, intention, and tone, to name only a few
- ☐ To keep a record of things

- ☐ To write books, poetry, or exams, for example
- ☐ To inform
- ☐ To create advertising material
- ☐ To tell stories
- ☐ To create programs
- ☐ To set goals
- ☐ To create affirmations
- ☐ To counsel

The importance of words and their impact on ourselves, our environment and life itself is quite evident. Everything in our world came to be by the use of words and images.

The words we use every day are the means by which we program and/or condition our life. What we think, say, and do in this moment determines what we experience every day because we can only create in the present moment. So, for me, the power of our words and the images they create are utterly important. The more powerful the words are, the more powerful the images and vice versa. The selection of powerful words and images is conducive to a feeling of confidence in achieving personal mastery. It allows us to live an extraordinary life in service to the universal intelligence for the highest good of all.

How we live, move, and have our being in this world depends on how we use our words and translate them into actions that are beneficial for each and every one of us. We have a responsibility to be fully conscious of our thoughts, words, actions, and deeds. Individually as well as collectively, our words constitute a power house.

In our communication, it is essential that our words convey the meaning we wish to impart. If we considered our words as elixirs, we would constantly be refining our communication skills. We would truly say what we mean and mean what we say. Our communication would be clear and pure and our words absolutely empowering.

Confucius once said: "Put mind in gear, before putting tongue in motion." This wisdom is noteworthy. How often have we heard the saying: "Think before you speak"? Putting this wisdom into practice translates into a more meaningful conversation as everyone who is listening receives the quality of our time, effort, and ingenuity. It also allows for a more captivating conversation and gives it a quintessential quality. Our conversation becomes the perfect embodiment of our breath because it expresses our essential truth. The breath we inhale, exhale, and use to communicate is Divine in nature.

Words have a powerful and transforming effect in that they can contribute to a more peaceful existence, optimal health, and well-being. They also enable us to become responsible citizens of the universe, thereby creating a much better environment in which to live, move, and have our being.

Accordingly, understanding the meaning of our words is paramount to making ourselves understood.

To be fully responsible for the words I use, I investigate what each word stands for in order to create a vocabulary that reflects my intention and the proper meaning I wish to convey. The following quote from an unknown author makes this point: *"A word is the final expression of a thought on the physical plane and, in other words, a word is a final creative act; and the word that you or I use is really indicative of our state of consciousness."*

INVESTIGATION

To understand the true meaning of the words we use, I have found it useful to investigate their derivation. The three sources I use are these:

1. *The Random House Dictionary of the English Language,* Second Edition (Unabridged)

2. *The Synonym Finder* by J.I. Rodale and Nancy LaRoche

3. *Roget's International Thesaurus,* Fourth Edition by Robert L. Chapman

By doing this, I have learned that there are many ways in which to express a certain word depending on the context or idea I wish to convey. The art of communication can be very artistic and powerful. It opens the doorway to a mutually beneficial experience. As an example, let's see what our sources have to say about the definition of the word *word*.

From *The Random House Dictionary* a *word* is defined as follows:

A unit of language, consisting of one or more spoken sounds or their written representations that function as a principal carrier of meaning.

From *The Synonym Finder* a *word* is defined as

☐ A term
☐ A name
☐ An expression
☐ An ideogram
☐ A hieroglyphic

From *Roget's Thesaurus* a *word* is
- ☐ An affirmation
- ☐ An account
- ☐ A command
- ☐ An information
- ☐ A unit of meaning

If we were to look up each word on the list, we would see that there are many more meanings. It would certainly be an education, some of which could be quite surprising. It was discovered that certain words show up where you least expect them to be.

When we understand the meaning behind words, they have much more power. The energy projected will be true to form and credible.

This may seem like a lot of work; however, I assure you it is a worthwhile endeavor. Like any formula, the more we use it, the faster we become familiar with it as we know exactly what we're looking for. Sometimes it helps to affirm the choice of the words we wish to use, much like creating a masterpiece if that is what we want to achieve.

Someone once said we only get out of life what we put in, or what we put out comes back. So it is best to know what we are putting out, to know what will come back. The meaning and intent of our words will be reflected in what comes back. It is important that we are clear in our communication at all times.

Looking at definitions can also assist us in determining an intention, which is the subject of our next word.

INTENTION

An intention according to *The Random House Dictionary* as defined as this: "An act or instance of determining mentally upon some action or result."

The intention behind the use of a word determines the cause and the emotions we invest, which propel us into action. Quality words and images, along with the intention, are the ingredients needed to set us on a path to acquiring the skill and knowledge necessary to manifest our objectives.

When we are in a creative mode, we are actually fully present utilizing our emotional energy properly. Our emotional energy is the fuel we apply to propel an action. The Divine Presence supplies the aspiration to activate the emotional response necessary that will lead us into action. We usually feel excited, pumped up, confident, and daring. We feel alive and connected with the Divine Presence that is expressing through us. In essence, we are fulfilling our purpose as agents of the Divine Consciousness.

Our ability to use high-quality words and intentions produces high-quality imagery. This reflects the excellence and ingenuity that is being expressed to the degree that we understand the aspiration originally transmitted.

Whatever the result, we will know the cause and source of what we've put into play, how it was organized, and the strategy used in mapping the big picture, which ultimately produces the end result. The buck starts and stops with us, so to speak, as we will be the recipient at some point in time of what we have put into play.

If we like the end result of the formula we used, we know that we have made an appropriate choice and have impressed properly upon our subconscious mind (more on this later). In that case, we can say that the inner and outer pictures are in harmony and congruent in nature.

Our intention creates an intonation pattern and the sound produced through our voice, which is the subject of our next word.

INTONATION

We are all very aware of the tone in which something is expressed. This tone can have such a profound effect on us and this tone can make or break our day. It tells us a great deal about whom we're communicating with, what frame of mind they are in, and whether we will even participate in the conversation.

Words produce a sound; therefore, the tone of the person speaking to us helps or affects greatly our ability to listen, hear, and interact with that person. We want our words to produce a melody enjoyed by our listeners.

Just think of all the music produced today. What makes us buy a certain song? Is it the wording that stirs us? Is it the images that come to mind by the words being sung?

I have observed many singers who are so attuned to the words and the music they produce that it feels as if they have reached a rapturous state. Perhaps we buy their records because deep emotions are touched within us, which we enjoy and want to recapture.

When we attend a lecture and the intonation of the speaker is a monotone, we stop paying attention. On the contrary, when a lecturer is animated, we feel enlivened, inspired, and fully captivated.

The meaning and intent behind our words create a tone that produces a feeling. For example, the word *love* is tossed around a great deal. Let's look at the meaning and intent behind the word *love*.

If the meaning of love for some is blind as in the cliché, "Love is blind," what would the sound of this person's voice reflecting this cliché produce within us? What would we experience upon hearing that love is sublime if the meaning and intent were exaltation, nobility, and inspiration?

When people are fully attuned to what love means for them, their behavior is animated when they speak the word, and the sound and meaning of love will most likely reverberate more deeply within the listener as well as within the speaker.

If meaning, intention, and intonation can have a profound effect on us, what will the power of suggestion do? We explore this in our next word.

SUGGESTION

We are always subjected to the power of suggestion. To give a short example: A friend gives you a recipe for a delicious cake. You're excited about tasting this cake because your friend is so ecstatic in her description of its taste that you want to get started right away to have the same experience. In the next breath, your friend says: "Be careful about doing this; watch out for that and if you do this, this will happen; if you do that, the result will be different." All of a sudden, something diminishes your enthusiasm because the suggestion implanted intimates that success is questionable. So your initial desire to try the recipe has suddenly faded.

The image and mind-set we have determine our level of success. The more we reinforce a successful outcome, the more confident we are of experiencing this delicious cake with absolute delight. With such a frame of mind, we are better prepared to reach the desired intention.

If there was ever any question about the power of suggestion, just look at the advertising industry, the news industry, the magazine industry, and the number of books written, bought, and sold. The combinations of words and pictures are used strategically to capture our attention with the hopes that we will purchase what is offered. We are made to feel that we need what is being advertised or expounded upon to improve the quality of our life.

In the same way, I am hoping that you will consider the ideas I am presenting useful enough to apply and, hence, improve the quality of your life.

What about the power of subliminal messages? On that subject, here's what *The Random House Dictionary* says: "adj. Psychol. Existing or operating below the threshold of consciousness: being or employing stimuli insufficiently intense to produce a discrete sensation but often designed to be intense enough to influence the mental process or the behavior of the individual."

Whether the suggestion is overt or subliminal, the power is the same. It employs stimuli to influence the mental process and/or behavior of the individual. Just watch a hypnotist in action. They employ the power of suggestion brilliantly.

The power of suggestion can govern how we think, feel, and act. Being conscious of what we take in requires diligence on our part to maintain a state of equilibrium.

Think about the power of suggestion in the language used to describe the following ideas about learning to control your mind and pay particular attention to how you think and feel afterward. (This excerpt is taken from *How To with Self-Hypnosis,* by Stephen Steiner).

"By learning to control your mind, you can find the power to deal with whatever situation arises, rather than allowing yourself to be thrown by it. Are you facing a problem that seems overwhelming and insurmountable? Tell yourself that impossibility is the escape of a small man's mind. Don't let anxiety paralyze your thinking processes, but instead think carefully and consider the problem. Assess the situation. Think about how best to handle it and make your decision. It's far better to take a chance on being wrong than to do nothing at all."

Now, let's look at this, written differently. Focus on how the present moment could be and, as I mentioned earlier, pay particular attention to how you think and feel afterward.

By learning to control your mind, you have the power to deal with whatever situation arises. Assess the situation and think carefully considering what is before you. Ask yourself the best way to handle it to make your decision. It is better to go for it and see what wisdom you gain from the experience to add to your wealth of knowledge.

Which option do you think will work best for you?

How can anyone feel confident about the resolution of a situation while concerned about being thrown by something that is overwhelming and insurmountable with the possibility of having a small man's mind experiencing anxiety?

I have come to understand that my experience may differ from someone else's. If we both do the same thing, we can attain different results. The reason for this is that our inner programming is made up of the words and the images we focus on along with the intention behind it all.

We are the only ones who truly know what is right for us. Our conditioning determines how we think, feel, and act. The words and images we use are the tools used to express that conditioning.

If the result is other than desirable, change the words and images communicated to the subconscious mind to produce a more desirable result, which is the subject of our next word.

Communication

Thoughts

- ☐ To articulate our thoughts and images, we need to use words as the impact our words have is determined by everything we have discussed thus far.

- ☐ Our thoughts can be expressed in written form and conveyed through various mediums such as advertising, news, magazines, books, songs, paintings, and poetry, to name a few.

Words In Print

Being mindful of the written word is primary to us as the power of suggestion is very strong. Our truth may differ from someone else's because truth is always subject to our own perspective on life and how we think it works. So it is wise to pay attention to the suggestive power of our words.

Words We Hear

What about the words we hear? There is always a possibility that we might have a different understanding of the meaning that someone else wants to convey and therefore would miss what is being said. If that is the case, it is best to ask for clarification to make sure we understand the intended meaning.

When the tone of voice is less than desirable, our listening ability is often turned off. We may be able to smile and nod at the most precise times during the course of such a conversation. In doing so, we make the speaker feel that we've been involved in the conversation the whole time when, in fact, we have been everywhere else except present.

Transposition of Words

During the course of my own restructuring, I had to learn how to transpose in my mind certain words or phrases spoken by others, in order to stay focused and present in a conversation. There is an association we have to words that can transport us out of the present moment and into memory. Our mental attitude can be changed immediately if we allow ourselves to follow these associations thereby changing our receptivity to the conversation we are in at the time. There are many opportunities to practice the art of transposition as you will see from the following.

What Is and What Isn't

I have become exceptionally aware of how explanations of what something is can usually be described by what it isn't. As an example, let us look at the definition of the word and color *red*.

According to Wikipedia on the Internet: "Red is any of a number of similar colors evoked by light consisting predominantly of the longest wavelengths of light discernible by the human eye, in the wavelength range of roughly 625–740 nm. [This is what *is*.] Red is also one of the subtractive primary colors of RYB color space [This is what *is*.] but not CMYK color space." [This is what *isn't*.]

"The RYB color space is RYB (an abbreviation of red-yellow-blue) and a historical set of subtractive primary colors. It is primarily used in art and design education, particularly painting. It predates modern scientific color theory." [What *is*.]

From what is and what isn't, the power of suggestion is at play. I would now have to investigate the CMYK color space to find out what that *is*. While this may add to my wealth of knowledge, it is a hindrance to me right now as it is taking me off track.

Here's what Wikipedia says about CMYK color space.

"CMYK (short for cyan, magenta, yellow, and key (black) and often referred to as process color or four color) is a subtractive color model used in color printing also used to describe the printing process itself. Though it varies by print house, press operator, press manufacturer and press run, ink is typically applied in the order of the abbreviation.

"The CMYK model works by partially or entirely masking certain colors on the typically white background (that is, absorbing particular wavelengths of light). Such a model is called *subtractive* because inks 'subtract' brightness from white."

Now that we've taken the route of learning what red is and isn't, I ask, what possible relevance does the CMYK color space have to do with red? Red is a subtractive primary color, and CMYK is a subtractive color model. Their only connection is that they are both of a subtractive nature. Their functions are totally different. If I were writing about subtractive elements, then all of this has relevance.

To stay focused on the original subject, which is red, is to write about what is relevant to red. Look at the time I could have saved if I did just that. In order to reacquaint myself with the original intent, I would have to reread it to get back on track.

On that note, I offer the following:

"Red is any of a number of similar colors evoked by light consisting predominantly of the longest wavelengths of light discernible by the human eye, in the wavelength range of roughly 625–740 nm. Red is also one of the subtractive primary colors of RYB color space. The RYB color space is RYB (an abbreviation of red-yellow-blue) and a historical set of subtractive primary colors. It is primarily used in art and design education, particularly painting. It predates modern scientific color theory."

Writing about what red *is* took thirty-four words to describe instead of the nearly one hundred words it took to write about what red *is* and *isn't*.

Now that you have read through what is and isn't, how did that process make you feel now? I know I was affected by this and had to clear my mind to continue writing.

What *isn't* takes me away from my primary focus, which is describing what *is*. Something else has been added to the mix, which in most cases can cause a change of interest.

What *is*, has to do with what's happening right here, right now. Expressing what is, keeps us fully present. Everyone's interpretation of what *is* may differ. However, this is a method in which we can learn that there are many ways something can be expressed or presented, which expands our knowledge and which is positive in nature.

POSITIVE AND NEGATIVE WORDS

I have also become very aware how the positive of anything is usually expressed using negative words. Here are just a few examples:

FIRST EXAMPLE

I love you not because of who you are, but because of who I am when I am with you. How does this make you feel?

Here's probably what the person wanted to say: I love you because of who I am when I am with you.

For me this is much more empowering to both parties.

SECOND EXAMPLE

Just because someone doesn't love you the way you want them to, doesn't mean they don't love you with all they have.

Perhaps the intent here is that those who love me, love me with all they have.

THIRD EXAMPLE

Don't waste your time on a man/woman who isn't willing to waste their time on you.

Perhaps the most empowering response could be: I spend my time wisely.

You may think that the examples using negative words are still of a positive nature, but the creative mind, as I have heard, skips by the negative word and focuses on the rest. That being the case, then let's look at our example of don't waste your time on a man/woman who isn't willing to waste their time on you.

If the creative brain skips by the words *don't* and *isn't*, then the focus is on wasting time on a man/woman who willingly wastes their time. What kind of a relationship is this to have? Better yet, what will ever be accomplished?

How often have we told others don't do this and don't do that and wonder why they do it? The answer is their brain interpreted the command as—do this and that—the very thing you asked them not to do. This creates challenges for both parties and strains relationships.

The following is a statement I found using positive words: "A true friend is someone who reaches for your hand and touches your heart."

So many elements are involved in our everyday communication. To be effective communicators, we are required to think before we speak. It is essential for us to be fully mindful and present, observing, listening, and hearing so that we are able to respond in a way that serves the highest good. This leads us into another area of communication that has to do with how we talk to ourselves.

We are usually mentally talking to ourselves about one thing or another. We are constantly critiquing ourselves as well as others. How often do we praise ourselves for a job well done? Our abilities and capabilities are determined by our thoughts, words, actions, and deeds. Whatever we're thinking, saying, and doing, fifty trillion cells are listening and participating, according Dr. Jill Bolte Taylor, author of *My Stroke of Insight*.

If we tell ourselves

☐ That we can do something, then we can and our subconscious mind will see to it that we are supplied with what is needed to accomplish the task.

☐ That we enjoy optimum health and well-being, can you imagine what our fifty trillion cells will do to achieve optimal health and well-being?

☐ That we can achieve anything we set our mind to, then that will be the result. It may take time; however, it will come to pass. Time prepares us to step into our new reality.

The choice is always ours to make. Our life is ours to design. The quality of the program we use to design our life determines its outcome.

It all starts with a thought, an idea, or a pattern. Our words produce images, signs, and symbols. They say a picture is worth a thousand words. If we occupy our mind with empowering images, keeping our focus on them, then, at a point in time called *now*, the outer picture matches the inner picture.

We are the architect and designer of our life, using a simple tool called words that produce a corresponding image. Our life is always a work in progress, and our words are an instrumental mechanism. As mentioned earlier words are the major building blocks of the events in our lives.

To be fully congruent in our verbal and body language, it is strongly suggested to know the true meaning we want to impart to make sure it brings out the best in us.

Being mindful requires that our mind does what we want it to, which is the subject of our next word.

MIND

Mind is the master weaver, both of the interior garment of character and the outer garment of circumstance. — James Allen

The mind is the medium through which our thoughts, ideas, and images appear. It's like a computer monitor or television screen. We have the ability to control what appears on this screen like selecting a channel to watch on television. Depending on which level of our mind we're tuning into will ultimately decide what will show up on the screen. To my understanding, the mind has three major components: the super-conscious, the self-conscious and the subconscious

THE SUPER-CONSCIOUS REALM

The super-conscious mind can be called by many names: God, universal intelligence, universal mind, higher self, the life force, consciousness, and the field of all possibilities, just to name a few.

All that comes to us comes from this level. It is what gives life to everything. It's what inspires us to be creative as that is our inherent nature.

Many books and schools of thought are devoted and dedicated to the understanding of this realm, so my aim is to keep it as simple as possible.

To access this realm, we must be fully present. When we are fully present, we become one with this mind, and we are then transported beyond our personality or ego level of existence. We are unified in every way—the ultimate place to live, move, and have our being.

The Self-conscious Realm

- ☐ It receives information from the super-conscious mind.
- ☐ It is the mediator between super-conscious and subconscious.
- ☐ It has the power to control the subconscious mind.
- ☐ It must be in the present moment to receive the information.
- ☐ It has to be fully present to create, ponder, or change anything.

The self-conscious mind is our personality and the vehicle for the life force to operate through. Being fully present is a must if we want to be in a receptive state.

The self-conscious mind is quite powerful and must be used wisely.

Our self-conscious mind has the ability to program and influence the subconscious mental realm. There is a saying out there that goes like this: "Be careful what you ask for as you are likely to get it." This is quite true. Here is where our words have the greatest impact.

The Subconscious Realm

- ☐ Is intelligent and creative
- ☐ Is amenable to suggestions
- ☐ Is highly impressionable
- ☐ Is a part of the universal mind
- ☐ Is the seat of habit according to Charles Haanel
- ☐ Is the storehouse of all memory

The information received by the self-conscious is processed by the subconscious realm where

- ☐ It is sifted, sorted, categorized, and made ready for use at anytime.
- ☐ It informs us where to obtain what we need in order for some of our goals to be manifested.
- ☐ It guides us to the right place at the right time to do the right thing facilitating the manifestation process.
- ☐ It educates us based on our operative programming.

How we talk to ourselves programs us. Everything we think, say, and do programs us for that matter. The subconscious mind records everything, every single detail of our life. The results of what we hear, smell, taste, touch, and feel along with our thoughts about it are recorded and archived for future use.

All of our beliefs, opinions, rules, regulations, strengths, and virtues are also recorded.

All these things are key factors in our ability to manifest. How we've been conditioned in life will determine the quality of our life. We are all effective and proficient as the architect and designer of our life. If we want more out of life, then we have to upgrade or change the existing program.

If our subconscious mind is allowed to take full direction from the super-conscious mind, then life works as if by miracles. To do this requires a complete reconditioning of the self-conscious mind to do what it was designed to do, which is to be the mediator between the super-conscious and subconscious mental realms—the vehicle (body) and agent.

The subconscious mind must also be put back on its original program, which is akin to the super-conscious mind. This requires great trust on the part of the self-conscious mind as it has been in control for a long time. By reconditioning the self-conscious, the subconscious automatically overwrites the old program. The end result is that all three levels of mind are singing from the same song sheet.

When the self-conscious impresses goals and intentions by way of repetition, reinforcement, and visualization on the subconscious mind and it takes hold, then all that we think, say, and do starts operating according to the goals and intentions we've programmed. The super-conscious directs and activates the subconscious processes instantly. The subconscious receives the command in its full content. That is why what manifests is usually better than what we think or could possibly plan. When this happens we usually say, *Wow, this is so much more than I could have ever dreamed of.*

In summary, I'd like to use an analogy for the super-conscious, self-conscious and subconscious mentality.

The super-conscious mind is like a candy store that has everything you could possibly ever want or need. The self-conscious mind is the child coming into the candy store salivating. The child wants everything in this store and wants it *now* (ego). The parent is the subconscious mind letting us have what has been allowed for in our programming.

Another analogy is this: The super-conscious is the Chairman of the Board, the self-conscious is the CEO, and the subconscious is the Manager in charge of production and results. The Manager will produce only to the quality of instruction provided for by the CEO. The CEO can only give the quality of instruction based on the understanding he or she has about the instruction given primarily from the Chairman.

The ultimate is that the CEO allows the authentic information transmitted by the Chairman to proceed directly to the Manager. In order for this to happen, the self-conscious must be the silent observer allowing the transmission to go directly to the subconscious. The subconscious, in turn, will give the CEO the information necessary to accomplish the task transmitted by the Chairman at the most precise time.

Imagine for a moment the self-conscious mind as the body. The super-conscious is the motivating force and the subconscious is the mapping system. The super-conscious says to subconscious:

There is a need to go downtown to get such and such, and it needs to happen at this time. The subconscious receives the information and begins to source out the best place and route to achieve the intended goal. The idea of going downtown to get such and such along with the destination and route to take is then transmitted at the precise time specified by the super-conscious to the self-conscious. The self-conscious then programs the route into the car's GPS system to get to the appropriate store. All is set and ready to go. The self-conscious turns the ignition key in the car and drives to the intended destination programmed into the GPS system and accomplishes the task. This scenario shows the ultimate team working together harmoniously.

If you want excellence, then let the Divine Presence come through and guide. This is such a transformative process. It is like being taken care of in every way imaginable. It has our best interest at heart. The guess work is alleviated; however, full trust is required. To help us in developing that trust, the Divine Presence uses a mirroring system, the subject of our next word.

MIRROR

The Divine Presence has and uses a mirroring system. Life is the medium used to mirror for us exactly what is going on inside and outside of us. It lets us know if we are hitting the mark in various ways such as situations, circumstances, events, people, animals, and sounds, to name a few.

The Law of Correspondence states: "As above, so below; as below so above; as within so without; as without so within" *(The Kybalion)*.

"As above, so below" means that the lower mirrors the upper, which means that our body is the printout of what's going on in our mind and vice versa (our abilities and capabilities, state of health, and so forth).

"As within, so without" means that in order for us to know what is going on in our inner world (mind), we need to look at what is being mirrored by our outer world (life), and vice versa.

I have found that using the mirror concept in my everyday life was instrumental in my ability to change. I recognized that everything in life mirrors one thing or another.

People reflect back to us elements of our self. It is the most useful tool for self-improvement that I know of today. If we're happy, someone will reflect this back. If we're persistent, this will be reflected back. As a matter of fact, everything we think, say, or do is reflected back to us through various mediums—the most effective being people and nature.

During my own process of reprogramming, mirroring was highly powerful to say the least. If I was having a challenge with anyone, I would stop and ask myself what that person was reflecting back to me. I soon realized that the specific thing I was reacting to was the very thing I was doing to someone else in an area that I needed to become conscious of. As soon as I made this discovery, all emotional attachment to any reaction miraculously vanished, and I was left in a state of well-being, very grateful to the messenger.

When Stephen Steiner introduced me to the mirror exercise, I found it intriguing. I soon discovered just how powerful and effective it was.

This exercise has four components to it:

1. Concentration
2. Conditioning
3. Reinforcement
4. Visualization

Here are just a few benefits derived from this mirror exercise and the possibilities for improvement if used:

☐ The ability to concentrate and focus on one thing at a time for an extended period of time

☐ The unity of mind and body since both are needed to do this exercise

☐ The promotion of conscious participation

☐ The ability to become aware of just what is going on in your mind

☐ A greater awareness of everything you think, say, and do

☐ A greater ability to be with yourself for an extended period of time and to feel comfortable in your own skin

☐ An ongoing and strengthening ability to stay in the present moment for an extended period of time in order to deliberately use your reasoning and intuitive abilities to bring yourself to a state of understanding

☐ A greater understanding of your place in the grand scheme of things

I present the mirror exercise next. It is my sincere hope that you will try it and realize how powerful and beneficial this tool is to improve the quality of your life.

Mirror Exercise

1. The mirror I use is 15.5 inches in diameter. It is circular and is placed about 6 inches above eye level. Place a round spot about 1.5 inches in diameter in the center of the mirror. The idea is to gaze upward at the spot so that your eyes are more easily fixed in place.

2. Angle the mirror in such a way that it reflects a blank area. You may have to tilt the mirror toward the ceiling. All you should see in the mirror is a white spot to captivate your attention.

3. Now that the mirror is positioned and ready, sit down in your chair about an arm's length away from the mirror and put both feet flat on the floor and rest your hands leisurely on your lap.

4. Relax, inhale, and exhale very deeply three times. Then continue to breathe more naturally.

5. Center your attention on the spot. You can repeat the word *spot* to yourself in your mind to keep your attention completely on the spot.

6. The instant you find your thoughts drifting, stop for a moment, stand up, and start again with three breaths. Stopping insures that your mind and body remain 100 percent focused. In other words, you are disciplining your mind and body to stay in the here and now in order to expand your concentration span and your ability to stay present.

7. At this point, I recommend that, in the time you stop, you can implement with passion one of your new paradigms. Sit back down and start again taking three deep breaths and direct yourself to the spot and repeat the word *spot* in your mind. Continue this process for ten minutes. For the remaining five minutes, get a mental image of yourself embodying all of your new paradigms and focus on this image for five minutes with your eyes closed using the same procedure (visualization). If your mind and body wander, stop and repeat another one of your paradigms, sit back down, take three deep breaths, and focus on the image again.

8. The key to reprogramming or implementing new consciousness is repetition, patience, and perseverance.

9. Do this exercise for at least fifteen minutes each day. If time permits, doing it twice a day increases your ability to be in control of your mind and what's in it. It also gives your mind a rest. In the morning you could start your day with a focused mind and at the end of the day you could go to sleep with a clear and focused mind. How much time you spend in this exercise is ultimately up to you. Do what you feel is best at all times.

This exercise is vital to developing two of the most important assets you have: your mind and your body. Spend the time now in its development, and your mind and body will pay dividends forever.

When doing this exercise, you may have some realizations. Write them down as they are significant to your ability to come to terms with certain situations in your life or to make life-altering change.

The benefit of expanding your concentration is the subject of our next word.

CONCENTRATION

The first component to the mirror exercise is to continually cultivate, develop and strengthen your ability to concentrate.

Each moment of pure concentration perpetually accumulates. Each time you sit down to do the mirror focus exercise, you start accumulating mind and willpower that builds each and every day. Your mind and body get stronger, better, and more efficient. As a result, your ability to concentrate is much stronger, and your ability to focus for extended periods of time increases.

Concentrating on your goals or images is impressing on the subconscious mind.

The same principle applies to muscle building. When you exercise your muscles, there is also a cumulative effect every time you exercise them. They get stronger. Consider your brain a muscle and build it as strong as possible. The stronger the muscle, the more power it has. Each thought now has an accumulated power, which allows for penetrating projection into the infinite reality for manifestation.

There is also a calming effect to this exercise. To be able to use your concentrated mind and body on a subject for an extended period of time allows you to investigate, learn from, and utilize information to maximize your potential. This helps in the decision-making process. When making an important decision, you have to spend considerable time deliberating so that you can use sound reasoning to sift and sort the information to make an informed decision.

The conditioning program you implement in order for your mind and body to work is vital to the life you live. It is the working mental software that tells your mind and body how you want them to work for you—kind of like a job description, the subject of our next word.

CONDITIONING

The second component to the mirror exercise is to plant the seeds of new paradigms, affirmations, goals, and aspirations.

The only time anything can be created, changed, or acted upon is in the here and now. I need to be here to hear and see any communication coming from the infinite realm or the field of all possibilities so that I will know what action needs to take place now, in order to manifest my goals.

When creating a new mental software conditioning program, you must make sure the words you use are positive and empowering. Remember as I wrote earlier, you are writing a job description, so to speak, to give to the subconscious. A reference back to the word *communication* will refresh your memory concerning this information.

In essence, the conditioning program you give to your subconscious mind becomes the mental software program that works through the motherboard called the brain. It is a master computing system.

Careful thought and consideration has to go into the creation of your mental software program because you will be the recipient of it. Situations, circumstances, events, people, places, and things will be presented to you each day to get a feel for how this is working for you. Therefore, each day affords you the opportunity to learn, grow, and upgrade the operating system. Each day becomes the canvas upon which you, as the chief designer and engineer, can make the changes you see fit to accomplish. Your life then becomes much more meaningful.

If your desire is to manifest yourself as a truly spiritualized human being and responsible citizen of the universe, you will have to determine the type of software that will be needed to eat, breathe, walk, and talk this type of being. Being present and hearing what this is from the Divine Presence will be an all-encompassing factor. What is needed can be something totally different than what you think, so you must be open and willing to implement what comes from the Divine Presence, even if it sounds ludicrous.

Here is just a small example of how the message can sound ludicrous. One day I was working in my office in the lower level of my home, and I asked my self to let me know when my brother-in-law was coming to the door as our doorbell was hard to hear in the lower level. As I was working away, I received this message: Go and check the door knob upstairs. I said to my self, the door knob is working fine. The message repeated, and I said okay, I will go and check. As I had thought, the door knob was working fine on the inside, so I decided to check it on the outside.

When I opened the door, my brother-in-law was standing there waiting to knock on the door as he was unaware of where the doorbell was. After that I followed the directions given, even though they might lead me to a place with a dead end. It might have been necessary to put me out of harm's way or at a different point in time.

For me a spiritualized human being means embodying the attributes of the Divine Presence. This insures that we can become effective vehicles for the Divine Presence to experience and express itself.

This is an evolutionary process. We are already doing it at some level. We need to be more conscious of this process in order to refine our physical being to express more of this Divine energy into the world. A greater awareness is necessary to make it so.

As an example of this I will share the basic foundation of the mental software program I implemented for becoming a spiritualized human being—a responsible citizen of this universe and an effective agent for the Divine Presence.

☐ I am I, the master self, a focalized center of power manifesting and expressing the ultimate power in its manifestations and expressions in the universe.

This affirmation helps us to understand our place in the scheme of things and puts the spiritual element at the forefront. It embodies the hermetic saying, "As above, so below; as within, so without." Through a process of investigation, we internalize that we are indeed an expression and agent for the Divine Presence or consciousness that is in and behind all life and form.

☐ I am the master of my life, every moment of every day as I take full charge of my mind and body, giving the appropriate direction to maximize my infinite potential.

To be an effective agent for the Divine Presence, we must be the master of our life at all times. It is our responsibility. Therefore, we must be conscious of everything we think, say, and do as it has a huge impact on all life and the world we inhabit. Life teaches us very quickly what it takes to achieve this level of mastery.

☐ I am an able, capable, self-confident, self-reliant, forward-looking, happy, responsible, calm, relaxed, and positive. People believe in me because I believe in myself and *I love life*.

With this affirmation, we are giving our subconscious mind a description of who we are as an agent for the Divine Presence. Therefore, all of our thoughts, words, actions, and deeds must reflect that we are able, capable people.

☐ I activate and generate the brilliant and effective use of my creative imagination.

In any situation we are faced with, our creative imagination supplies the images needed. This enables us to think on our feet at a moment's notice. Our creative imagination is a precious asset, one that should be continually cultivated, developed, strengthened, and utilized.

☐ I brilliantly harness, mobilize, and utilize my creative intelligence, gift of reason, and free will in every way, every day.

This is how our brain will organize itself. We are asking for the highest and best to achieve the highest and best possible result to maximize our infinite potential.

☐ I brilliantly implement, exercise, and maximize my wealth of knowledge in every way, every day.

Here, we indicate to our subconscious mind what information to access to achieve the desired aim. Our wealth of knowledge lies in the wisdom we have acquired through our life experiences. We operate from our sense of knowing.

☐ I put my mind in gear before putting my tongue in motion.

If we think before we speak, we are thereby harnessing all of the previous attributes effectively and efficiently for the highest good of all.

☐ The actions I perform are brilliantly intelligent, creative, and effective, in harmony with my true spiritual nature and conducive to the growth, development, and well-being of all.

This becomes a parameter for all my actions in order to be a responsible citizen of the universe and true agent for the Divine Presence.

☐ I choose to conduct my life in a compassionate way using a high level of personal mastery every moment of every day for the highest good of all.

To be a compassionate and empathetic human for me denotes true humanitarianism—a true gift indeed!

As you can see, I have used the word *brilliant* in my mental software repeatedly. I wish to draw the best of what I am able and capable of. Also for me, brilliance comes from the Divine Presence that resides within each and every one of us. When we are in the midst of brilliance, it is proof enough that the Divine Presence is truly expressing itself.

The repetition of these paradigms gradually translates into an incentive to emulate the Divine Presence to the degree that we know and understand all of its attributes. Because my true aim is to become a spiritualized human being, a true agent for the Divine Presence, I wish to be a clear pathway for the Divine Presence to express itself in this world.

To put our software to work immediately, consider these three words that are of great import. They are *from now on.* The instruction to the subconscious mind is that *from now on* we are the master of our life as able, capable people. We have the brilliant and effective use of our creative imagination, harnessing our creative intelligence, gift of reason, and free will. We implement our wealth of knowledge in ways that are in harmony with our true spiritual nature. We conduct our life in a compassionate way using a high level of personal mastery to serve the greatest good of all.

From now on also signifies that the present moment is brand new and full of infinite possibilities to explore and learn from.

It kind of reproduces the idea behind the commercial on a product called Bits and Bites—a trail mix. It shows that each handful presents a new combination to enjoy. *From now on* creates a new experience that adds to our storehouse of knowledge, which is always at our disposal. *From now on* can give us a feeling of a fresh start as it means that from now on we are looking forward to a new reality.

We can continually upgrade our mental software program just as computer software is upgraded. Today's programs become obsolete the moment they hit the stores. The programmers continually see how the program can work better, faster, and more efficiently.

"That a man can change himself, improve himself, re-create himself, control his environment, and master his own destiny is the conclusion of every mind who is wide-awake to the power of right thought in constructive action." — From The Master Key System.

Remember, the more seeds you plant, the more flowers will grow and bloom given the right soil and nutrients. The continual watering of these seeds is of a repetitive nature, the subject of our next word.

Reinforcement

As the third component of the mirror exercise, reinforcement is a key factor in implementing a new mental conditioning program. It is imperative that the reinforcement methods used be effective, because the strength of the impression made on the subconscious mind provides a quicker activation. In other words, the better the impression made, the faster the result.

Imagine the power of the sun focused through a magnifying glass atop a sheet of paper. When the focus is strong enough and long enough, a hole will burn through the paper.

I asked my self to provide me different ways in which to do this. This is what came:

One day, the thought of singing my goals came, another day I would act them out, and yet another day, I would simulate ownership by walking and talking my goals the way I thought an able, capable, self-confident, self-reliant, forward-looking, happy, responsible, calm, relaxed, and positive person would walk and talk. Reinforcement can only happen when we are in the now.

The day I realized that my thoughts were either in the past or the future, I decided to reinforce being in the now by repeating the words *in the now* as a mantra every chance I got. It became a challenge sometimes to stop saying it as these words became so automatic.

License plate numbers brought me in the here and now. This made sure that I was focused on my driving. The subconscious will produce many different ways in which to bring us into the present. When you're on the road and someone moves in front of you abruptly and forces you to apply your brakes, this is a sure sign that you were elsewhere in your mind if it produced a reaction. This happened to make you conscious of your surroundings.

I remember once, I was walking toward hypnotherapist Stephen Steiner's office, and the voluminous shape of a person's hair caught my attention. It reminded me of a vision I had. I was so involved with the person's hair that I almost walked into a cement lamp post. (This is an example of the power of association that I mentioned earlier in the discussion of the word *communication*.)

So if your goal is to be fully present, rest assured that the subconscious will see to it that you are made aware of the present in whatever means that it can to get your attention.

Just saying three simple words *in the now* brought me a wealth of knowledge, truth, and wisdom. I also realized my place in the scheme of creation and just who has the power. The only thing I can control is my mind and what I create in the here and now.

Reinforcement is a determining factor to the reconditioning process just as the sun's light reflects through the magnifying glass onto the paper, which represents the subconscious mind.

The power of visualization is also a way to reinforce our new mental software, the subject of our next word.

VISUALIZATION

We have now come to the fourth and pivotal component to the mirror exercise and the use of our creative imagination.

Using our creative imagination is essential to the process of manifestation. For the most part words come from the left part of our brain and the images from the right part of our brain. This is why the remaining five minutes of the mirror focus exercise is spent on the visualization aspect. Five minutes is a minimum. I have found that sometimes when I focus on seeing myself as the person embodying the new program, I would make adjustments to the picture I was focusing on. I would add details, make it sunny, see colors, and bring in a favorite aroma. I would also visualize myself interacting in everyday life, walking, talking, breathing, eating, laughing, running, and enjoying my new world.

This image would come to my mind easily. Even a few seconds expended multiple times a day is worthwhile. We are happiest when we are being creative, like children making castles in the sand. We are so blessed to have such a magnificent mental function called the creative imagination.

Creating a desire through imagery reminds me of a television ad in which a gentleman is celebrating his birthday and making a wish. The image of the car he wants comes up and brings a smile to his face. In the next scene, he is sitting on a park bench and becomes aware of a four-leaf clover. While holding the four-leaf clover, the image of the car comes to his mind, and another smile lights up his face. He then gets up from the bench and starts walking along and sees a penny on the ground. As he picks it up, the image of the car comes into his mind. There is a sense of luxury in his smile, and the next thing he knows he is being handed the keys to this car. A desire manifested.

That is what it takes: the reinforcement and repetition of focusing on the image until it becomes manifest. How the wish comes true is in the domain of the Divine Presence. All we have to do is to accept the gift with gratitude.

This image becomes the mold or template for what is to materialize. The mental focus is filling the template or mind with the energy of creation. When the template is fully charged with energy, it becomes material. Manufacturing plants show this process very well. It all starts with words, which produce pictures and vice-versa.

If we are happy with the finished product, then we celebrate the attainment. If we say *I wish it could be more like this or that,* then we have to add something to our creative process and upgrade the software program. Changing the picture and instructions changes the end product.

"The vision always precedes and itself determines the realization." — Lillian Whiting

The only time that we can do this is in the *now*, the subject of our next word.

Now

Anything that has ever been manifested was created in the *now*. All the power that ever was, is, or will be is here *now*. The *now* is infinite and eternal in nature. It is the field of all possibilities. All is contained in the *All*. The past and future reside in the *now*, so for me, there is only *now*. It is the only thing that is real.

To create, contemplate, or change anything, we must be in the *now*. Everything resides and manifests in the *now*. When we have the eyes to see and the ears to hear, we can then know what needs to be created, contemplated, or changed. Constant communication is happening. We receive a great deal of information when we are in the *now*. It is vibratory in nature, which becomes processed by our mental faculties and results in thoughts, ideas, inspiration, and motivations.

One day I was stopped at a busy intersection waiting for the light to turn green. In that moment, I noticed how all the cars came together precisely then and also that everything was changing at such a speed it was hard to keep up. I asked my self at the time, *how would I ever be able to do this with such precision?* I realized in that moment, the power of *now*—my place in the grand scheme of it all and how much can be learned from what is shown to us by this Divine Presence, when we are fully present.

Now is the field of all possibilities, the infinite and eternal realm. *Now* is when I am fully connected to the infinite, so whatever I can do to stay here and now maintains my connection to the field of consciousness.

We, like batteries, are recharged in the *now*. Just sitting quietly and focusing on the sound of silence is a great way to recharge. It is like having a cat nap, so to speak. When we are participating in the *now*, we can be animated and expanded because we are beyond our personality. We are inspired, full of ideas, confident, motivated, and raring to go.

In the *now*, we are beyond time and space. We just *are*. When we are back into our personality and look at our watch, we see that five hours has passed, and it seemed like only a few minutes.

Being in the *now* requires our full participation. Being in that space can make us feel whole and complete. The self-conscious mind has joined forces with the super-conscious and the subconscious realms.

Now spelled backward is *won*. Also if you just heard the word *won*, you might think of the word *one* or see the numeral one (1).

What have we won being in the *now*? Oneness with all there is, because we made *now* the one and only priority.

When we experience this, we have reached attainment—the subject of our next word.

ATTAINMENT

People over the years have found formulas for creating and attaining results. I present to you a Master Formula of Attainment from *The Personal Power Series* written by two scholars, W.W. Atkinson and E.E. Beale, back in the early 1900s. I spent a lot of time with this formula a number of years ago. It states simply what is required to complete any project.

THE MASTER FORMULA OF ATTAINMENT

The Master Formula of Attainment consists of five elements:
1. Definite Ideals
2. Insistent Desire
3. Confident Expectation
4. Persistent Determination
5. Balanced Compensation

The master formula may be expressed as follows: You may have anything you want, providing that you
1. Know exactly what you want.
2. Want it strongly enough.
3. Confidently expect to obtain it.
4. Persistently determine to obtain it.
5. Are willing to pay the price for its attainment.

It is important to realize that we manifest all the time. Becoming aware of how we do it so that we can make our life easier is the true secret to becoming the best we can be living the life of our choosing and to attain whatever our heart truly desires.

I came across another formula of attainment that I found equally as good. It is called the 4D Habit (author unknown). It reinforces the desire to be very productive with new and existing positive habits. It says that in order to do so we must

1. *Decide* to plant and implement new positive habits, thoughts, ideas, and ideals to best achieve our goals and aspirations.
2. Take immediate action by *doing* it now.
3. Be *determined* to see it through.
4. *Deepen* our resolute commitment to succeed.

You can have the Master Formula in place, but it is necessary to make a decision to implement it.

I added these formulas to my mental software program by using them as the following goals:

- ☐ My ideals are definite in nature.
- ☐ My desire is insistent.
- ☐ I have confident expectation.
- ☐ I have persistent determination.
- ☐ I have balanced compensation.
- ☐ I know exactly what I want.
- ☐ I desire what I want strongly enough.
- ☐ I confidently expect to obtain the desire.
- ☐ I persistently determine to obtain the desire.
- ☐ I am willing to do what is necessary to attain the desire.
- ☐ I *decide* to plant and implement new positive habits, thoughts, ideas, and ideals to best achieve my goals and aspirations.
- ☐ I take immediate action by *doing* it now.
- ☐ I am *determined* to see it through.
- ☐ I *deepen* my resolute commitment to succeed.

In reinforcing these goals each day, forces are set in motion to continually cultivate, develop, and strengthen my ability to create and manifest the highest and best for the highest good of all.

I also found that in order to achieve anything we need the three *P*s: patience, persistence, and perseverance. Right now everything that is happening in our life took time to achieve. It will take time for the new conditioning program to overwrite the old program.

As an example: Let's plant a seed in our garden. We take special care to prepare the soil for our seed to take root. We water it and nourish it with our love, looking forward to seeing it bloom. The next day, the child in us asks *is it ready yet?* So we dig up the earth covering our seed to see if it has taken root and grown. How fast do you think this will take to grow and will the seed survive the constant light of day? We must exercise patience because we know that nature takes its course.

We must be persistent in our endeavor to see it bloom by nurturing it with water and the love of our desire to see it bloom. Lastly, we must persevere through the times when our patience is challenged.

At times when I wanted it all to happen right now, this minute, I would repeat the following statement over and over again, *I can, I will, I dare, I do,* with great intensity. It changes my mental state as it forces me to be in the here and how. It reinforces my desire to be victorious because I know that I can, I am willing to attain, I dare to attain, and I do attain. This bijou came from the *Personal Power Series* for which I am also grateful. It helps tremendously.

I would put as much power as I could into this declaration to bring me back to being patient, persistent, and persevering in my endeavor to attain.

When we're faced with trying situations, we can also use this gift from Eckhart Tolle's book *A New Earth*: "and this too shall pass."

Another way I used words to stay present and moving forward to attainment was creating an oracle, using word cards.

One of the most important features of using this process for me is the establishment of an inner communication with the Divine Presence within, as I am seeking its counsel.

Many years ago, I used to frequent New Age bookstores. I was fascinated by tarot cards or any type of cards that were of a divining nature. One day I happened to come across a box of word cards. They were called the Words of Truth. I immediately bought them and started working with them. They led me on a journey that has brought about the writing of this book.

There were two hundred cards in all, both positive and negative words. I reached the point where I was becoming apprehensive about picking these words, as I was concerned about picking the negative words, which affected my mental state. So I decided to take out all of the negative words and replace them with more empowering words. I have been continually cultivating these word cards for over twelve years.

Whenever I was having a trying day, I immediately consulted my word cards to find out what I was really dealing with. Because I was using only positive words, I discovered that I needed to learn how to handle the positive aspects of my life. Since the *now* is brand new and full of infinite possibilities I now had to interpret what the Divine Presence was showing me in a more empowering way. This took some time; however, using the word cards helped enormously in this process. It opened up new ways to look at different situations and at life as a whole.

The words I picked were so on the mark that I was astounded. The fact that they were picked at random was even more remarkable. I would ask questions and pick a word. Sometimes I would have a number in my mind and pick that number of words. I arranged these words in a way that made a sentence or paragraph. The message became clear, and my direction was such that I knew what I had to do to achieve a resolution or a course of action.

Most of the time, the message melted away the emotional charge and left me feeling much better and more relaxed. Once my frame of mind was set on a higher track, I would feel exhilarated and encouraged that I had found an answer. For this I am forever grateful to the Divine Presence within for having put me on to this tool as a medium of communication and counsel.

I decided to make up a few sets of word cards and give them to people that I knew and ask them to try them out to see what results they got. I present two examples of the feedback I received just recently.

"I know that when I address the highest within me with a sincere question, and then dig into the bag of cards and extract one that seems to be the first one I comfortably hold on to with my fingers, the perfect word and thought presents itself. Sometimes I will then ask for further understanding and draw another card. Almost always brilliant new thoughts add to the initial ones—like intuitive impressions that can sometimes flow during a good meditation.

"At first I thought this a strange and neat coincidence. I now realize that deep laws within the subconscious mind are being activated, leaving no room for chance.

"In confidently trusting the source of my being to guide me, methods such as this help me to strengthen the two-way communication between me and that inner or higher self. I draw a card every morning and include its thoughts in my meditations and preparations for the day. I receive both warnings of what to expect and guidance on how to conduct myself. I have stopped being surprised, sometimes astounded, at the accuracy and direction I receive and have developed more of an awareness, appreciation and love of that source.

"When studying or practicing a spiritual exercise, the cards enhance or add deeper understanding for me. They help broaden my perspective during troubling times, they help with decision making, with lending thoughtful and meaningful assistance to others, and with generally bringing peace of mind. No question seems too petty or too grand. I have even found humor and gentle reprimand coming forth!"

Here is the second comment I received: "In general, I just pull a word in the morning and that word will tell me what I might expect for the day. The day will present tons of opportunities for me to express that particular word, or perhaps how I should conduct myself. I save my words for a week, and I have noticed a pattern in the week. For example, suppose I pulled *commitment* on a Monday. The words for the balance of the week will relate. Like pulling a general and then fleshing that first one out … rather like a painting."

I am grateful for this feedback because it shows me that this technique will work for anyone who uses this system.

I made up cards with sayings on them. So I had a bag of plain words and a bag of affirmations, goals, and aspiration cards. Then one day, I had the idea of putting the ideals and goals on the back of the word card. Taking two sets and making them one. This was reinforcing the ideals and goals that were most apropos for the day in question. Every time I read a book and come across an ideal that I liked, I made it part of my working mental software conditioning program.

My word cards were transformed into words of wisdom cards. I gave a set of these to a dear friend, and he shared with me how he used them at Christmas time. He would pick a word card for each person he was sending a Christmas card to and would write the words of wisdom that were on the back of the word card. He was astounded as to what the response was. Everyone said how timely it was to receive this important message. They all said that the Christmas card had much more meaning to it because my friend took the time to think just about them and offer a gift of loving kindness. This was music to my ears. I was very grateful that it increased the level of humanity for all concerned.

There are many different ways to maintain the state of patience, persistence, and perseverance. It is valuable to find whatever works to get us back into the present moment where everything is as it is.

Finally, how do we know that we have been successful in our attainment? Well, for one, when the inside and outside pictures match. We have a feeling of unity, completion, and fulfillment. We are satisfied. Why? Perhaps because the inside and outside pictures are representative of our personality merging into the infinite and eternal where we are one. It makes us feel that what was transmitted from the Divine Presence was fully understood and received and the requirements met. Perhaps that is truly why we want to go for the gold. It is a symbol of the highest vibration—one in which we want to live, move, and have our being.

Second, we are living the life we truly want to live and being the person we truly want to be.

Third, we are relating to everything around us in a noble way. We continually cultivate, develop, and strengthen a sustainable abundance of wealth for the purpose of empowering and endowing humanity and all life. This allows us to intelligently manage all of the earth's resources for the highest good.

The entire universe is always ready to assist us. We just have to enlist its help, which is accessed in the present moment.

When we are calm, relaxed, and patient, we are truly in a receptive state to stop, look, listen, and act in accordance with our highest ideals for the greatest good of all.

Epilogue

The power of the mind is infinite and eternal in nature. We have the capability of developing it to whatever capacity we desire.

Through self-reprogramming we can effectively change our lives and mold them to reflect our true hearts' desire.

Life is a great teacher as it sets up all the avenues in which to test our resolve to be the best we can be—to be more than we were a moment ago.

All this can come about by implementing a few simple phrases made up of empowering everyday words.

BIBLIOGRAPHY

Atkinson, W.W. and E.E. Beale. The Personal Power Series.

Bolte Taylor, Jill. *My Stroke of Insight: A Brain Scientist's Personal Journey.* New York: Viking, 2008.

Braden, Gregg. Walking Between the Worlds: The Science of Compassion. New York: Radio Bookstore Press, 1997.

The Gospel According to St. John, chapter 1, first line of the Holy Bible, King James Version. (http://etext.virginia.edu/toc/modeng/public/KjvJohn.html)

Haanel, Charles. *The Master Key System.* Originally published 1917, current updates available. (ebook available for free download at www.haanel.com)

Smith, Patrick. *The Emerald Tablet of Hermes Trismegistus.* Sequim, Wash.: Holmes Publishing Group, 1997.

Steiner, Stephen. *How To with Self-Hypnosis.*

Three Initiates. *The Kybalion: A Study of the Hermetic Philosophy of Ancient Egypt and Greece.* Chicago: Yogi Publication Society, 1912. (www.kybalion.org/kybalion.asp)

Tolle, Eckhart. *A New Earth: Awakening to Your Life's Purpose.* New York: Penguin, 2008.

About the Author

My name is Liz McGrath. I have been married to my husband Gerry for forty-three years. We have two amazing daughters named Jeanette and Shar, a great son-in-law named Harry and three wonderful grandchildren—Shanelle, Liam, and Shane.

We live in Thornhill, Ontario, Canada. Our life has led us into many arenas, and we've taken a few roller-coaster rides. Some of them were very scary.

Life has been my greatest teacher as my schooling only prepared me for being a nurse, a secretary, a receptionist, or a typist in the working world.

Life is a most exacting task master which forced me to rely on my ingenuity while paying attention to my inner self to reach solutions and resolutions. It is a most humanizing process and experience. Because of this we had to live by our wits at times, which led us into areas of learning that showed us how best to handle these situations.

By following these ways, we have effectively changed the course of our lives for the better.

Life has led me to this moment in time and the writing of this book.

For your information:

I can be reached at: liz@thepowerofourwords.com

My website is: http://www.thepowerofourwords.com

The word cards mentioned in this book can be purchased at: www.thepowerofourwords.com